Alfred's Basic Piano Library

Piano

Classic Themes
Level 3

Allan Small

This book contains new arrangements of great *Classic Themes*. Many of these beautiful melodies were not originally written for the keyboard. Composers write music in many instrumental forms—symphonies, concertos, ballets, etc. Allan Small has taken some of the most popular and arranged them in graded order for the piano student. Also included are arrangements of vocal music. There is music from popular operas as well as folk music, music that was passed down from one generation to another and whose composers are frequently unknown.

The purpose of this series of *Classic Themes* is to allow the piano student to become familiar with these beautiful melodies by performing them. Though not in any way a substitute for the original composition, *Classic Themes*, through its arrangements and

write-ups for each selection, will give the student a heightened awareness of many composers and their works. By performing these arrangements and by listening to the recordings of the compositions in their original form, the student will gain an expanded understanding of and appreciation for the truly great music of the past.

The four books of *Classic Themes*, Levels 2–5, are designed to supplement ALFRED'S BASIC PIANO LIBRARY and are coordinated page-by-page with the LESSON BOOKS. The instructions in the upper right corner of the first page of each piece clearly indicate when the student is ready to learn the piece. The pieces may be played at any time after the designated pages are covered, but it is best not to attempt them sooner than these references indicate.

2

Use after WALTZ PANTOMIME,
LESSON BOOK 3 (page 10).

Johann Strauss, Jr. (1825–1899) was known as the "Waltz King" because of the beauty and popularity of his many waltz compositions. Two of his better-known light operas are "The Gypsy Baron" and "The Bat" (*Die Fledermaus*). *The Beautiful Blue Danube* is probably the world's most famous waltz.

Blue Danube Waltz

Johann Strauss, Jr.

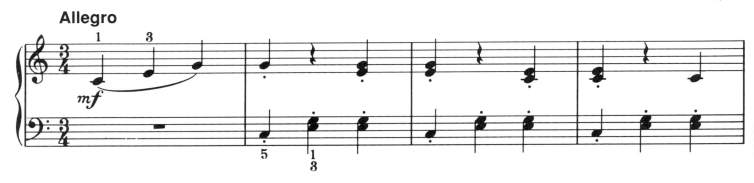

Play RH one octave higher on the repeat.

Use after WALTZ PANTOMIME (page 10).

Valse Lente
from "Coppélia"

Leo Delibes (1836–1891) was a French composer who is best known for his two ballets, "Coppélia" and "Sylvia" (see page 11). *Valse Lente* is taken from the comedy-ballet "Coppélia."

Leo Delibes

*Change fingers while sustaining the C.

Play both hands one octave higher on the repeat.

Use after PRELUDE (page 16).

This excerpt is taken from an overture based on an opera of the same name. The composer Otto Nicolai (1810–1849) is barely remembered today but his overture contains many happy themes and is a great favorite at concerts.

The Merry Wives of Windsor

Otto Nicolai

Flow Gently, Sweet Afton

Use after CHROMATIC SCALE (page 18).

This is a famous old English melody. The left hand denotes the gentle flow of the stream.

Traditional

Use after VILLAGE DANCE (page 19).

Jesu, Joy of Man's Desiring

This great melody written by Bach (1685–1750) flows smoothly with a peaceful and noble feeling.

**Moderato e tranquillo
(calmly)**

Johann Sebastian Bach

Pizzicati is the plural of *pizzicato*, which tells the string player to pluck the string with the finger instead of using the bow. This produces a short, dry sound. A pianist may imitate a pizzicato effect by playing staccato and omitting the pedal.

Pizzicati
from "Sylvia"

Leo Delibes

Sempre means *always*. Play both hands staccato throughout the piece.

Use after CASEY JONES (page 21).

Franz Liszt (1811–1886) was one of the outstanding pianists and composers of the 19th century. He wrote many Hungarian rhapsodies based on folk themes. His *Hungarian Rhapsody No. 2* is a thrilling piano composition, a great favorite of pianists and audiences everywhere.

Themes from
Hungarian Rhapsody No. 2

Franz Liszt

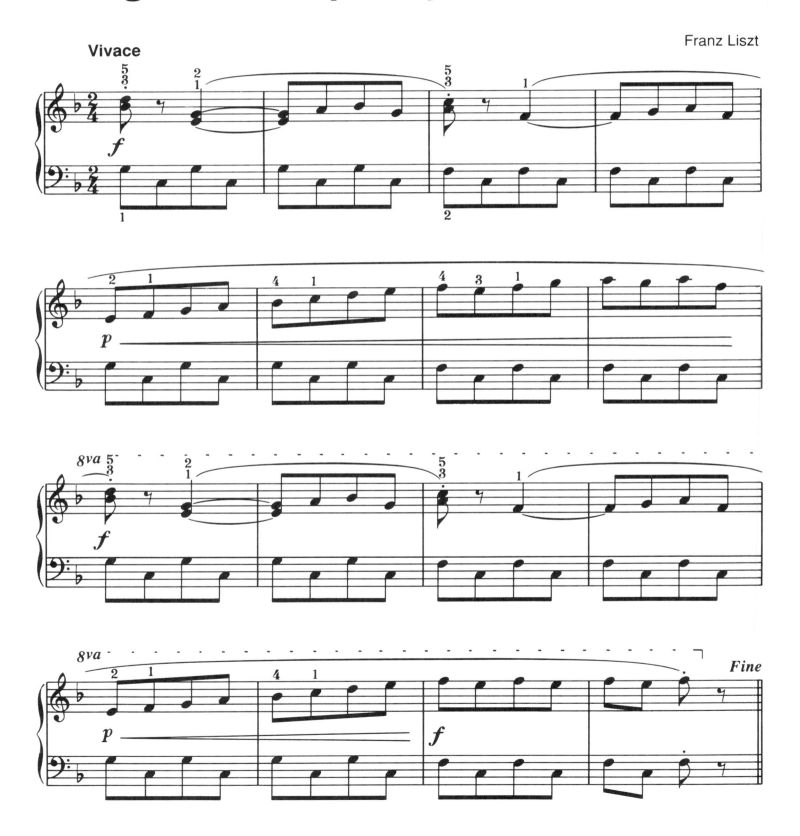

Use after A DAY IN VIENNA (page 22).

This is a popular Italian song. Play the long, melodic lines in the right hand with a warm, singing tone. The crisp left-hand staccato chords, which punctuate and add spice to the rhythm, contrast with the melody.

Ciribiribin

Albert Pestalozza

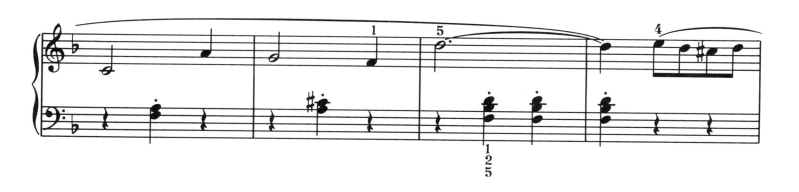

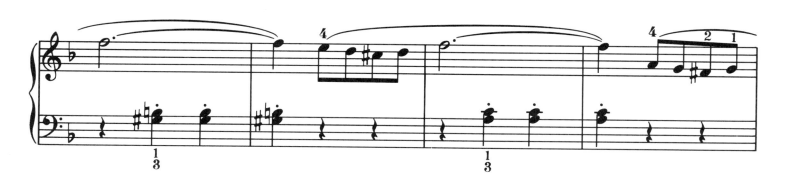

Play RH one octave higher on the repeat.

16

Use after A DAY IN VIENNA (page 22).

Englebert Humperdinck (1854–1921) became instantly famous because of his opera "Hansel and Gretel." For a while he was an assistant to Richard Wagner, one of the most influential composers of the 19th century.

Wooden Shoe Dance
from "Hansel and Gretel"

Engelbert Humperdinck

Play RH one octave higher on the repeat.

Use after A DAY IN VIENNA (page 22).

Auld Lang Syne

This is a favorite song in all English-speaking countries—especially at New Year's Eve.

Old Scottish Air

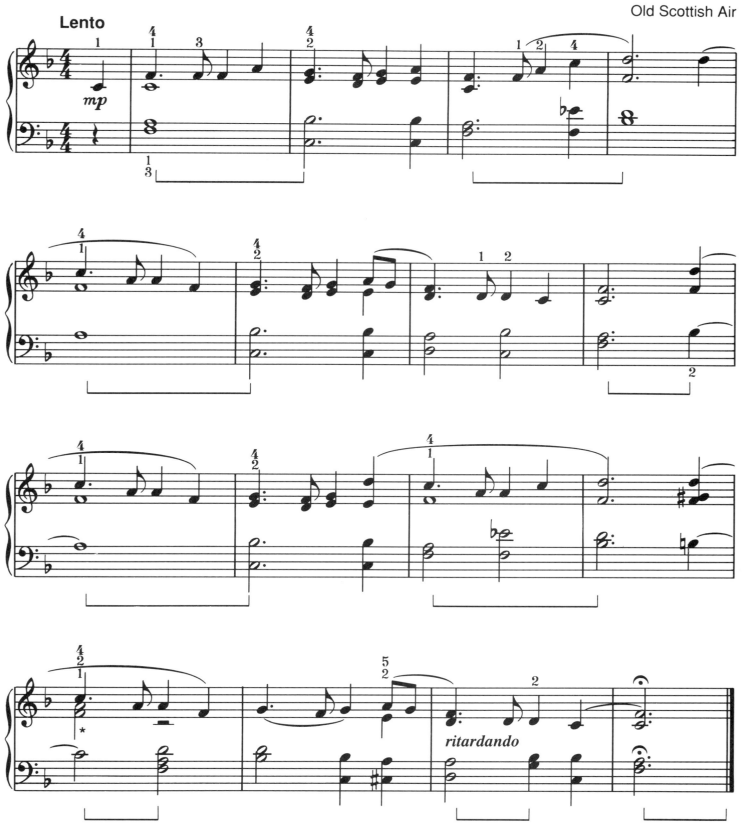

*The half notes are sustained by the pedal.

Russian Waltz

Use after ENCHANTED CITY (page 25).

This haunting waltz in A minor is a traditional Russian
tune that is still enjoyed by many dancers today.

Traditional

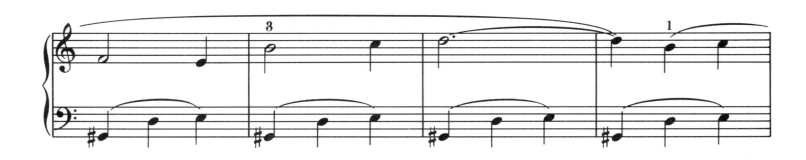

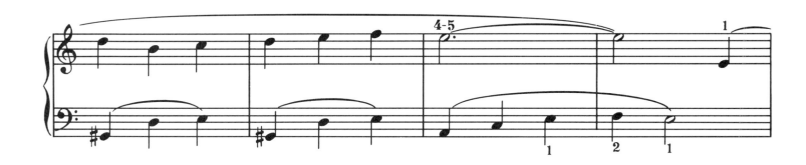

Play RH one octave higher on the repeat.

Use after MAKE UP YOUR MIND (page 27).

All Through the Night is a lovely and well-known lullaby. It is transposed from the
key of G major to C major the second time it is played, giving it a brighter feeling.

All Through the Night

Traditional

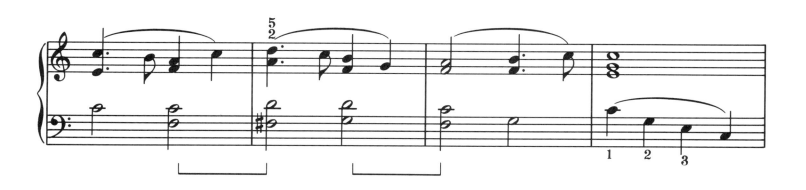

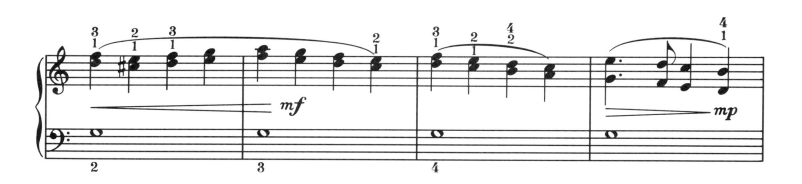

Use after THE MAJOR AND THE MINOR (page 28).

Pas d'Espagne is a lively European dance. The first section is in the key of C major while the second part, in a quieter mood, is in the relative key of A minor.

Spanish Dance
(Pas d'Espagne)

Traditional

D. C. al Fine

Use after GREENSLEEVES (page 30).

Chorale is one of a series of easy piano pieces by Robert Schumann (1810–1856). His wife Clara was one of the greatest pianists of the 19th century. He composed for her the famous *Piano Concerto in A Minor.* Robert also championed the young composer Johannes Brahms.

Chorale

Robert Schumann
Op. 68, No. 4

Use after GREENSLEEVES (page 30).

This is a cradle song. The piece consists of a melody with a lulling, rocking accompaniment.
The composer, Benjamin Godard (1849–1895), also wrote several operas and orchestral works.

Berceuse
from "Jocelyn"

Benjamin Godard

Andante e espressivo

Use after GREENSLEEVES (page 30).

Written by the Finnish composer Jean Sibelius (1865–1957), *Finlandia* is one of his best-known works. He won so much recognition as Finland's greatest composer that he was given a life-grant by the government.

Finlandia

Jean Sibelius

* D.S. (Dal Segno) means *from the sign.*

D.S. al Fine means *Repeat from the sign 𝄋 and play to the FINE.*

Use after RAISINS AND ALMONDS (page 40).

Dolores

Dolores is a beautiful and haunting waltz. Émile Waldteufel (1837–1915) was famous for writing the French waltz in much the same way as Johann Strauss, Jr. was for the Viennese waltz.

Émile Waldteufel

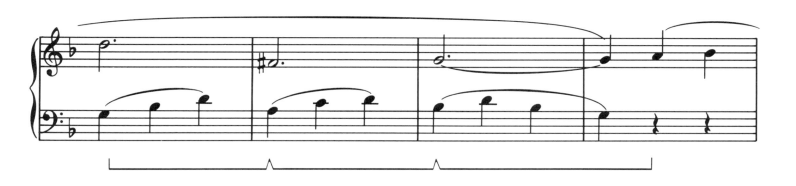

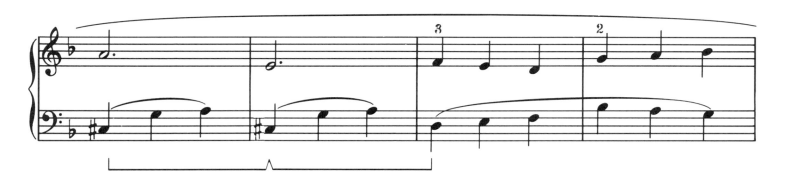

Use after RAISINS AND ALMONDS (page 40).

Israeli Dance

This lively dance is based on a traditional Israeli tune.
It is sung and danced at many festive occasions.

Traditional

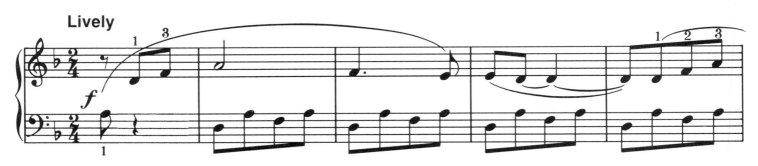

Use after LA RASPA (page 44).

Charles Gounod (1818–1893) was descended from a family of artists; his father was a painter. Gounod wrote music mainly for the theater, although he wrote several symphonies. His great success was the opera "Faust." *Funeral March of a Marionette* was used as the theme to a very popular mystery show on radio and television.

Funeral March of a Marionette

Charles Gounod